*No real gentleman
should be without
these rules for perfect conduct
first compiled in the 1890s.*

ETIQUETTE
for
GENTLEMEN

Copper Beech Publishing

This edition published in Great Britain by
Copper Beech Publishing Ltd

ISBN 1 898617 08 2

Photography: Allen Barnes
Cover Design: Geoff Gillard

Special thanks to Jan and Graham Upton at 'How We Lived Then'
Museum of Shops, Eastbourne, for permission to photograph their
collection of Victorian household objects.

Copper Beech Publishing Ltd
P O Box 159 East Grinstead
Sussex England RH19 4FS

"He's a gentleman: look at his boots."

From Pygmalion by George Bernard Shaw

INTRODUCTIONS

The chivalry of etiquette assumes that the lady is invariably the superior in right of her sex, and that the gentleman is honoured in the introduction.

To introduce persons who are mutually unknown is to undertake a serious responsibility.

Never undertake this responsibility without in the first place asking yourself whether the persons are likely to be agreeable to each other.

Always introduce the gentleman to the lady - never the lady to the gentleman. The chivalry of etiquette assumes that the lady is invariably the superior in right of her sex, and that the gentleman is honoured in the introduction.

Where the sexes are the same, always present the inferior to the superior.

Never present a gentleman to a lady without first asking her permission to do so.

When you are introduced to a lady, never offer your hand. When introduced, persons limit their recognition of each other to a bow.

Never introduce afternoon visitors who happen to encounter each other in your rooms. Visitors thus casually meeting in the house of a friend should converse with ease as if they were acquainted. To be silent and stiff on such an occasion would show ignorance and ill-breeding.

Persons who have met at the house of a mutual friend without being introduced should not bow if they afterwards meet elsewhere. A bow implies acquaintance; and persons who have not been introduced are not acquainted.

If you are walking with one friend, and meet with, or are joined by, a third, do not commit the too frequent error of introducing them to each other.

Introductions at evening parties are now almost wholly dispensed with.

Some old-fashioned country hosts yet persevere in introducing each new-comer to all the assembled guests, thus the last unfortunate visitor is in a singularly awkward position.

All he can do is to make a semicircular bow, like a concert singer before an audience, and bear the general gaze with as much composure as possible!

LETTERS OF INTRODUCTION

Let your note-paper be of the highest quality.

Do not lightly give or promise letters of introduction. Always ask yourself whether the person introduced will be an acceptable acquaintance to the one to whom you present him, and whether the pleasure of knowing him will compensate for the time and money which it costs to entertain him.

Those to whom letters of introduction have been given should send them to the person to whom they are addressed, and enclose a card.

Never deliver a letter of introduction in person. It places you in the most undignified position imaginable, and compels you to wait while it is being read, like a footman who has been told to wait for an answer.

If the receiver of the letter be a really well-bred person, he will call upon you, or leave his card the next day, and you should return his attentions within the week.

If, on the other hand, a stranger sends you a letter of

introduction and his card, you are bound by the laws of politeness and hospitality, not only to call upon him the next day, but to follow up that attention with others.

If you invite him to dine with you it is a better compliment to ask some others to meet him than to dine with him *tête-à-tête*.

Be careful at the same time only to ask such persons as he will feel are at least his own social equals.

A letter of introduction should be given unsealed, not alone because your friend may wish to know what you have said of him, but also as a guarantee of your good faith.

As you should never give such a letter unless you can speak highly of the bearer, this rule of etiquette is easy to observe. By requesting your friend to fasten the envelope before forwarding the letter to its destination, you tacitly give him permission to inspect its contents.

Let your note-paper be of the highest quality.

VISITING - AFTERNOON CALLS - CARDS

Never take favourite dogs into a drawing-
room when you make a morning call.
Their feet may be dusty or they may bark.

An afternoon call should be paid between the hours of 3 and 5.30p.m. in winter, and 3 and 6p.m. in summer. By observing this rule, you avoid intruding before the luncheon is removed, and leave in sufficient time to allow the lady of the house an hour or two of leisure for her dinner toilette.

Many ladies find it a convenience for themselves and their friends to have a regular At Home day and, when possible, an effort should be made to call on a lady on her 'day' as you are then sure of finding her in and ready to receive guests.

A good memory for these trifles is one of the hall-marks of good breeding.

Visits of ceremony should be short. Beware of letting your call exceed half an hour's length; it is always better to let your friends regret than desire your withdrawal.

Leave-taking cards have P.P.C. (*pour prendre conge*) written in the corner. Some use P.D.A. (*pour dire adieu*).

A gentleman's visiting card must bear his name in small Italian lettering. If he possess a title, it must precede the name; if not, simply 'Mr.' with his address and club in the left-hand corner.

If, when paying a call, the lady of the house is not at home, leave one card for the gentleman and one for the ladies of the house; if there is no gentleman, only one card need be left.

These cards should be placed on the hall table.

When a gentleman makes a morning call, he should never leave his hat or riding-whip in the hall, but should take both into the room. To do otherwise would be to make himself too much at home. The hat, however, must never be laid on a table, piano, or any article of furniture; it should be held gracefully in the hand. If you are compelled to lay it aside, put it on the floor.

Umbrellas should invariably be left in the hall.

Never take favourite dogs into a drawing-room when you make a morning call. Their feet may be dusty, or they may bark at the sight of strangers, or, being of too friendly a disposition, may take the liberty of lying on a lady's gown, or jumping on the sofas and easy chairs. Where your friend has a favourite cat already established before the fire, a battle may ensue!

If, when you call upon a lady, you meet a lady visitor in her drawing-room, you should rise when that lady takes her leave, and escort her to her carriage, taking care, however, to return again to the drawing room, though it be only for a few minutes, before taking your own leave. Not to do this would give you the appearance of accompanying the lady visitor; or might, at all events, look as if the society of your hostess were insufficient to entertain you when her friend had departed.

If other visitors are announced, and you have already remained as long as courtesy requires, wait till they are seated, and then rise from your chair, take leave of your hostess, and bow politely to the newly arrived guests. You will, perhaps, be urged to remain, but, having once risen, it is always best to go. There is always a certain air of gaucherie in resuming your seat and repeating the ceremony of leave-taking.

If you have occasion to look at your watch during a call, ask permission to do so, and apologise for it on the plea of other appointments.

If he is escorting ladies, a gentleman must wait for them to terminate the call, and not rise until the ladies have done so.

CONVERSATION

*There is a certain distinct but
subdued tone of voice which is peculiar
to only well-bred persons.*

Let your conversation be adapted as skilfully as may be to your company. Some men make a point of talking commonplaces to all ladies alike, as if a woman could only be a trifler. Others, on the contrary, seem to forget in what respects the education of a lady differs from that of a gentleman, and commit the opposite error of conversing on topics with which ladies are seldom acquainted.

A woman of sense has as much right to be annoyed by the one as a lady of ordinary education by the other.

You cannot pay a finer compliment to a woman of refinement and esprit than by leading the conversation into such a channel as may mark your appreciation of her superior attainments.

In talking with ladies of ordinary education, avoid political, scientific, or commercial topics, and choose only

17

such subjects as are likely to be of interest to them.

Remember that people take more interest in their own affairs than in anything else you can name.

If you wish your conversation to be thoroughly agreeable, lead a mother to talk of her children, a young lady of her last ball, an author of his forthcoming book, or an artist of his exhibition picture.

Be careful, however, on the other hand, not always to make a point of talking to persons upon general matters relating to their professions. To show an interest in their immediate concerns is flattering, but to converse with them too much about their own arts looks as if you thought them ignorant of other topics.

Do not use a classical quotation in the presence of ladies without apologising for or translating it. Whether in the presence of ladies or gentlemen, much display of learning is pedantic and out of place.

There is a certain distinct but subdued tone of voice which is peculiar to only well-bred persons. A loud voice is both disagreeable and vulgar. It is better to err by the use of too low than too loud a tone.

We have known even ladies pride themselves on the saucy chic with which they adopt certain Americanisms and other cant phrases of the day. Such habits cannot be too severely reprehended. They lower the tone of society and the standard of thought.

The use of proverbs is equally vulgar in conversation; and puns, unless they rise to the rank of witticisms, are to be scrupulously avoided. There is no greater nuisance in society than a dull and persevering punster.

Never interrupt a person who is speaking. It has been aptly said that 'if you interrupt a speaker in the middle of his sentence, you act almost as rudely as if, when walking with a companion, you were to thrust yourself before him, and stop his progress'.

To listen well is almost as great an art as to talk well. It is not enough *only* to listen. You must endeavour to seem interested in the conversation of others.

If a foreigner be one of the guests at a small party, and does not understand English sufficiently to follow what is said, good breeding demands that conversation shall be carried on in his own language.

If upon the entrance of a visitor you carry on the thread of a previous conversation, you should briefly recapitulate to him what has been said before he arrived.

Always look, but never stare, at those with whom you converse.

In order to meet the general needs of conversation in society, it is necessary that a man should be well acquainted with the current news and historical events of at least the last few years.

NOTES OF INVITATION, ETC.

*Fancy papers, fantastic borders, and
dainty coloured wax are only admissable
in the desk of a lady.*

Notes of invitation and acceptance are written in
the third person and the simplest style.

All notes of invitation are now issued in the name of the
mistress of the house only, as follows:

*Mrs Norman requests the pleasure of Sir George and Lady
Thurlow's company at an evening party, on Monday 14th June.*

Others prefer the subjoined form, which is purchasable
ready printed upon either cards or note-paper, with blanks
for names or dates:

*Mrs Norman
At home,
Monday evening, June 14th.*

An At Home is, however, considered somewhat less stately than an evening party, and partakes more of the character of a *conversazione*.

A reply to a note of invitation should be couched as follows:

Mr Berkeley has much pleasure in accepting Mrs Norman's kind invitation for Monday evening, June 14th.

A gentleman should never use anything but plain note-paper. Fancy papers, fantastic borders, dainty coloured wax, and the like elegant follies, are only admissible in the desk of a lady.

Never omit the address and date from any letter, whether of business, friendship, or ceremony.

In writing to persons much your superior or inferior, use as few words as possible. In the former case, to take up much of a great man's time is to take a liberty; in the latter to be diffuse is to be too familiar. It is only in familiar correspondence that long letters are permissible.

To be prompt in replying to a letter is to be polite.

IN THE STREET

*In walking with a lady, take charge of
any small parcel, parasol, or book
with which she may be encumbered.*

A **well-bred man** must entertain no respect for the
brim of his hat. 'A bow,' says La Fontaine, 'is a note drawn
at sight.' You are bound to acknowledge it immediately,
and to the full amount.

The two most elegant men of their day, Charles the
Second and George the Fourth, never failed to take off their
hats to the meanest of their subjects. Always bear this
example in mind; and remember that to nod, or merely to
touch the brim of the hat, is far from courteous.

On meeting friends with whom you are likely to
shake hands, remove your hat with the left hand in order to
leave the right hand free.

If you meet a lady in the street whom you are
sufficiently intimate to address, do not stop her, but turn
round and walk beside her in whichever direction she is

going. When you have said all that you wish to say, you can take your leave.

If you meet a lady with whom you are not particularly well acquainted, wait for her recognition before you venture to bow to her.

If you are on horseback and wish to converse with a lady who is on foot, you must dismount and lead your horse, so as not to give her the fatigue of looking up to your level.

When you meet friends or acquaintances in the streets or public places, take care not to pronounce their names so loudly as to attract the attention of the passers-by.

If you should be smoking in the street when you meet a lady, and stop to speak to her, the cigarette or cigar must at once be thrown away.

*It is not enough that a man should be clever ... he must
above all else know how to enter a room,
how to bow, and how to dress.*

DRESS

A gentleman's coat should not fit too well.
To be fitted too well is to look like
a tailor's assistant.

It is not enough that a man should be clever, or well educated, or well born; to take his place in society he must be acquainted with all that this little book proposes to teach.

He must, above all else, know how to enter the room, how to bow, and how to dress. Of these three indispensable qualifications, the most important, because the most observed, is the latter.

A gentleman should always be so well dressed that his dress shall never be observed at all. Does this sound like an enigma? It is not meant for one. It only implies that perfect simplicity is perfect elegance, and that the true test of taste in the toilette of a gentleman is its entire harmony, unobtrusiveness and becomingness.

If any friend should say to you, 'What a handsome

waistcoat you have on!' you may depend that a less hand-some waistcoat would be in better taste.

Display, in short, is ever to be avoided, especially in matters of dress.

To be too much in the fashion is as vulgar as to be too far behind it. No really well-bred man follows every new cut that he sees in his tailor's fashion-book. Only very young men and those not of the most aristocratic circles, are guilty of this folly.

In the morning wear frock-coats, double-breasted waistcoats, and trousers of light or dark colours, according to the season.

In the evening, though only in the bosom of your own family, wear only black, and be as scrupulous to put on a dress-coat as if you expected visitors. If you have sons, bring them up to do the same.

For evening At Homes, dinner-parties, and balls, wear a black dress-coat, black trousers, black or white waistcoat, white cravat, white kid gloves, and thin patent-leather boots. A black cravat may be worn in full dress, but it is not so correct as a white one.

A tail-coat should be worn on all but informal occasions. A dinner-jacket may be worn for home or informal dinners, or when going to the theatre with men only.

A black tie should not be worn when dining out, and neither black nor white ties should ever be bought ready made. A double collar should not be worn with dress-clothes, neither should a watch-chain.

A handkerchief used in the evening must always be pure white.

Jewellery should be worn very sparingly, if at all. A set of good studs, a gold watch and chain, and one signet or plain ring, are as many ornaments as a gentleman can wear with propriety. Your studs, however valuable, should be small.

For daytime, in the park lounge suits, with bowlers, straw or Homburg hats, are worn in the morning, but after lunch a frock-coat or morning coat and silk hat must take their place. With a black frock-coat dark trousers should be worn. Brown boots must, of course, never be worn with a frock-coat.

In the country, even when paying a call, a tweed suit and bowler or straw hat is quite correct. In fact, except at weddings and perhaps on Sundays, a frock-coat and silk hat are never worn.

In town, gloves should be worn out of doors. A

stick may be carried, but not when going to church.

Very light-coloured clothes for morning wear are to be avoided, even in the height of summer; and fancy cloths of strange patterns and mixtures are exceedingly objectionable.

Coloured shirts may be worn in the morning; but they should be small in pattern and quiet in colour.

With a coloured shirt always wear a white collar.

If your sight compels you to wear spectacles, let them be of the best and lightest make, and mounted in gold or blue steel.

In these days of public baths and universal progress, we trust that it is unnecessary to do more than hint at the necessity of the most fastidious personal cleanliness.

The hair, the teeth, the nails, should be faultlessly kept; and a soiled shirt, a dingy pocket-handkerchief, or a light waistcoat that has been worn once too often, are things to be scrupulously avoided by any man who is ambitious of preserving the exterior of a gentleman.

RIDING AND DRIVING

If the lady be light, take care not to give her
too much impetus in mounting. We have
known a lady nearly thrown over her horse
by misplaced zeal of this kind.

The rule of the road in riding and driving is to keep
to the left in meeting, and to the right in overtaking, another
vehicle or rider.

If you assist a lady to mount, hold your hand at a
convenient distance from the ground, that she may place
her foot in it. As she springs, you aid her by the impetus of
your hand.

In doing this, it is always better to agree upon a signal,
that her spring and your assistance may come at the same
moment.

For this purpose there is no better form than the old
duelling one of 'one, two, *three*.'

When the lady is in the saddle, it is your place to find
the stirrup for her, and guide her left foot to it. When this

is done, she rises in her seat, and you assist her to draw her habit straight.

If the lady be light, you must take care not to give her too much impetus in mounting. We have known a lady nearly thrown over her horse by misplaced zeal of this kind.

In riding with a lady, keep on her right.

If a gate has to be opened, we need hardly observe that it is your place to hold it open till the lady has passed through.

If when riding or driving with a lady you desire to smoke, her permission must first be asked.

When in a carriage, the gentleman should alight first, in order to assist the lady.

A gentleman cannot be too careful to avoid stepping on ladies' dresses when he gets in or out of a carriage. He should also beware of shutting them in with the door.

MORNING AND EVENING PARTIES

*If you have occasion to use your handkerchief,
do so as noiselessly as possible. To blow
your nose as if it were a trombone
is a vulgarity scrupulously to be avoided.*

The afternoon At Home is a modern invention; it was unknown to our fathers and mothers, and even to ourselves, until within recent years.

An evening At Home begins about 9 o'clock p.m., and ends about midnight, or somewhat later.

Good breeding neither demands that you should present yourself at the commencement, nor remain till the close of the evening. You come and go as may be most convenient to you, and by these means are at liberty to present yourself at two or three houses during a single evening.

Always put your gloves on before entering the drawing-room, and be careful that there is no speck of mud upon your boots or trousers.

If you have occasion to use your handkerchief, do so as noiselessly as possible. To blow your nose as if it were a trombone, or to turn your head aside when using your handkerchief, are vulgarities scrupulously to be avoided.

Never stand upon the hearth-rug with your back to the fire, either in a friend's house or in your own.

Never offer anyone the chair from which you have just risen, unless there be no other disengaged.

Should an impromptu dance be got up after dinner at a party where no dancing was intended, be sure not to omit putting on gloves before you stand up.

It is well always to have a pair of white gloves in your pocket in case of need.

Even though you may take no pleasure in cards, some knowledge of the etiquette and rules belonging to the games most in vogue is necessary to you in society.

Never play for higher stakes than you can afford to lose without regret. Cards should be resorted to for amusement only; for excitement, never.

No well-bred person ever loses his temper at the card-table. You have no right to sit down to the game unless you can bear a long run of ill luck with perfect composure, and are prepared cheerfully to pass over any blunders that your partner may chance to make.

If you are an indifferent player, make a point of saying so before you join a party at whist or bridge. If the others are fine players, they will be infinitely more obliged to you for declining than accepting their invitation. In any case, you have no right to spoil their pleasure by your bad play.

Be scrupulous to observe silence when any of the company are playing or singing. Remember that they are doing this for the amusement of the rest, and that to talk at such a time is ill-bred.

In retiring from a crowded party it is unnecessary that you should seek out the hostess for the purpose of bidding her a formal good-night. By doing this you would, perhaps, remind others that it was getting late, and cause the party to break up.

If you meet the lady of the house on your way to the drawing-room door, take your leave of her as unobtrusively as possible, and slip away without attracting the attention of her other guests.

THE DINNER TABLE

Every man should carve, and carve well.

To be acquainted with every detail of the etiquette pertaining to this subject is of the highest importance to every gentleman.

Ease, *savoir-faire*, and good breeding, are nowhere more indispensable than at the dinner-table, and the absence of them is nowhere more apparent. How to eat soup and what to do with a cherry-stone are weighty considerations when taken as the index of social status!

An invitation to dine should be replied to immediately, and unequivocally accepted or declined. Once accepted, nothing but an event of the last importance should cause you to fail in your engagement.

Invitations to a large dinner-party should be sent out about three weeks beforehand. They are issued in the joint names of the host and hostess, usually on a printed card, thus:

Mr and Mrs............................
request the pleasure of
....
Company at dinner
on Tuesday June 16th
8 o'clock

4, Park Place   R.S.V.P.

Such an invitation must be answered in the third person.
Five or six days' notice is sufficient for a small friendly
dinner, the invitation being, of course, written in the first
person.

In declining an invitation you must always give your
reason for so doing.

To be exactly punctual is the strictest politeness on these
occasions. If you are too early, you are in the way; if too late,
you spoil the dinner, annoy the hostess, and are hated by the
rest of the guests.

❧

Some are of the opinion that in the question of a dinner-party 'never' is better than 'late'; and say that, if you do not reach the house till dinner is served, you had better retire and send an apology, and not interrupt the harmony of the courses.

When the party is assembled, the mistress or master of the house will point out to each gentleman the lady whom he is to conduct to table.

If she be a stranger, you had better seek an introduction; if a previous acquaintance, take care to be near her when the dinner is announced, offer your arm, and go down according to precedence of rank.

When the society is of a distinguished kind, the host will do well to consult Debrett or Burke, before arranging his visitors.

When rank is not in question, other claims to precedence must be considered. The lady who is the greatest stranger should be taken down by the master of the house, and the gentleman who is the greatest stranger should conduct the hostess. Married ladies take precedence of single ladies, elder ladies of younger ones, and so forth.

It requires some tact to distribute your guests so that each shall find himself with a neighbour to his taste; but as much of the success of a dinner will depend on this matter, it is worth some consideration. If you have a wit, or a particularly good talker among your visitors, it is well to place him near the centre of the table, where he can be heard and talked to by all. It is obviously a bad plan to place two such persons in close proximity. They extinguish each other!

A little consideration of the opinions and tastes of his friends will enable a judicious host to avoid the many quicksands!

The gentlemen who support the lady of the house should offer to relieve her of the duties of hostess. Many ladies are well pleased thus to delegate the difficulties of carving, and all gentlemen who accept invitations to dinner should be prepared to render such assistance when called upon.

To offer to carve a dish, and then perform the office unskilfully, is an unpardonable gaucherie. Every gentleman should carve, and carve well.

As soon as you are seated at table, place your table-napkin across your knees, and remove the roll which you find probably within it to the left side of your plate.

If the dinner begin with *hors d'oeuvres*, they may either be on the table when you sit down, or are handed round after. They consist, as a rule, of anchovies, olives, etc., or oysters. If the latter they must be eaten with the fork alone.

Do not be afraid to read the menu, which will be put near you.

As soon as you are helped begin to eat; or, if the viands are too hot for your palate, take up your knife and fork and appear to begin. To wait for others is now not only old-fashioned, but ill-bred.

Never offer to pass on the plate to which you have been helped. This is a still more vulgar piece of politeness, and belongs to the manners of a hundred years ago. The lady of the house who sends your plate to you is the best judge of precedence at her own table.

In helping soup, fish, or any other dish, remember that to overfill a plate is as bad as to supply it too scantily.

Silver fish-knives will now always be met with at the best tables; but where there are none, a piece of crust should be taken in the left hand, and the fork in the right. There is no exception to this rule in eating fish.

We presume it is scarcely necessary to remind the reader that he is never, under any circumstances, to convey his knife to his mouth!

❦

Always help fish with a fish-slice, and tart and puddings with a spoon, or, if necessary, a spoon and fork.

Asparagus must be helped with the asparagus tongs.

In eating asparagus, it is well to observe what others do, and act accordingly. Some very well-bred people eat it with the fingers; others cut off the heads, and convey them to the mouth upon the fork. It would be difficult to say which is the more correct.

Tarts and curry are eaten with a spoon and fork, but for all sweets, mince, rissoles, etc., and whenever it is possible otherwise, use a fork alone.

In eating stone fruit, such as cherries damsons, etc., put the stones out from the mouth into a spoon, and so convey them to the plate.

Certain wines are taken with certain dishes, by old-established custom - as sherry, or sauterne with soup and fish; hock and claret with roast meat; punch with turtle; champagne with whitebait; port with venison; port or burgundy with game; sparkling wines between the roast and the confectionery; madeira with sweets; port with cheese; and for dessert, port, tokay, madeira, sherry and claret. Red wines should never be iced, even in summer. Claret and burgundy are always slightly warmed; claret-cup and champagne-cup should, of course, be iced.

Instead of cooling their wines in the ice-pail, some hosts have of late years introduced clear ice to be put inside the glasses. This is an innovation that cannot be too strictly reprehended or too soon abolished. Melting ice can but weaken the quality and flavour of the wine.

Those who desire to drink wine and water can ask for iced water if they choose, but it savours too much of economy on the part of the host to insinuate the ice inside the glasses of his guests, when the wine could be more effectually iced outside the bottle.

A silver knife and fork should be placed to each guest at dessert.

It is wise never to partake of any dish without knowing of what ingredients it is composed. You can always ask the servant who hands it to you, and you thereby avoid all danger of having to commit the impoliteness of leaving it, and showing that you do not approve of it!

Never speak while you have anything in your mouth.

Be careful never to taste soups or puddings till you are sure they are sufficiently cool, as by disregarding this caution, you may be compelled to swallow what is dangerously hot, or be driven to the unpardonable alternative of returning it to your plate.

When eating or drinking, avoid every kind of audible testimony to the fact.

Finger-glasses containing water are placed to each person at dessert. In these you may dip the tips of your fingers, wiping them afterwards on your table-napkin. If the finger-glass and doily are placed on your dessert-plate, you should immediately remove the doily to the left of your plate, and place the finger-glass upon it. By these means you leave the right for the wine glasses.

Coffee and liqueurs should be handed round when the dessert has been about a quarter of an hour on the table. After this, the ladies generally retire.

Should no servant be present to do so, the gentleman who is nearest the door should hold it for the ladies to pass through.

When the ladies leave the dining-room, the gentlemen all rise in their places, and do not resume their seats till the last lady is gone.

The servants leave the room when the dessert is on the table.

*If you should unfortunately overturn or
break anything, do not apologise for it. You can show
your regret in your face, but it is not well-bred
to put it into words.*

Should you injure a lady's dress, apologise amply, and assist her, if possible, to remove all traces of the damage.

To abstain from taking the last piece on the dish, or the last glass of wine in the decanter, only because it is the last, is highly ill-bred. It implies a fear that the vacancy cannot be supplied, and almost conveys an affront to your host.

To invite a friend to dinner is to become responsible for his happiness so long as he is under your roof.

A dinner, to be excellent, need not consist of a great variety of dishes; but everything should be of the best, and the cookery should be perfect.

That which should be cool should be cool as ice; that which should be hot should be smoking; the attendance should be rapid and noiseless; the guests well-assorted; the wines of the best quality; the host attentive and courteous; the room well-lighted; and the time punctual.

*The chief matter of consideration
at the dinner-table - as, indeed, everywhere else
in the life of a gentleman - is to be perfectly composed
and at his ease. He goes through all the
complicated duties of the scene as if he were
'to the manner born.'*

STAYING AT A FRIEND'S HOUSE
BREAKFAST, LUNCHEON ETC.

*A gentleman visitor who does nothing but
idle about the house and chat with
the ladies is an intolerable nuisance.*

A visitor is bound by the laws of social intercourse to conform in all respects to the habits of the house. In order to do this effectually, he should inquire, or cause his personal servant to inquire, what those habits are.

To keep your friend's breakfast on the table till a late hour; to delay the dinner by want of punctuality; to accept other invitations, and treat his house as if it were merely an hotel to be slept in; or to keep the family up till unwonted hours, are alike evidences of a want of good feeling and good breeding.

At breakfast and lunch absolute punctuality is not imperative; but a visitor should avoid being always the last to appear at table.

No order of precedence is observed at either breakfast or luncheon. Persons take their seats as they come in, and, having exchanged their morning salutations, begin to eat without waiting for the rest of the party.

As regards morning and evening greetings it is quite impossible to lay down a rule, and one should as far as possible fall in with the ways of the house.

If letters are delivered to you at breakfast or luncheon, you may read them by asking permission from the lady who presides at the urn.

Always hold yourself at the disposal of those whose house you are visiting. If they propose to ride, drive, walk, or otherwise occupy the day, you may take it for granted that these plans are made with reference to your enjoyment. You should, therefore, receive them with cheerfulness, and do your best to seem pleased, and be pleased, by the efforts which your friends make to entertain you.

You should never take a book from the library to your own room without requesting permission to borrow it. When it is lent, you should take every care that it sustains no injury while in your possession, and should cover it if necessary.

A guest should endeavour to amuse himself as much as possible, and not be continually dependent on his hosts for entertainment. He should remember that, however welcome he may be, he is not always wanted.

During the morning hours a gentleman visitor who neither shoots, reads, writes letters, nor does anything but idle about the house and chat with the ladies, is an intolerable nuisance. Sooner than become the latter, he had better retire to the billiard-room and practise cannons by himself, or pretend an engagement and walk about the neighbourhood.

Those who receive 'staying visitors,' as they are called, should remember that the truest hospitality is that which places the visitor most at his ease, and affords him the greatest opportunity for enjoyment.

A visitor should avoid giving unnecessary trouble to the servants of the house, and should be liberal to them when he leaves.

A few hints on the question of tipping may not come amiss here.

Of course, the amount of the tips must depend upon the attentions that you have received from the various servants, also, to some extent, upon the size of the house in which you are staying.

At an ordinary house the housemaid should receive half a sovereign for a visit of three weeks, or, if the visit has only extended over two or three days, a few shillings.

The coachman also must receive two or three shillings. Of course, in the case of a shooting-party, a much larger tip – gold or even paper – must be given to the gamekeeper, and at a large house the butler and valet will both expect to be tipped.

A gentleman of moderate means, however, should not attempt to tip in the lavish manner of some wealthy men, nor will the servants expect him so to do.

On returning from a visit, do not on any account forget to write and thank your hostess for her hospitality; this note should be sent within two days of your return.

GENERAL HINTS

*A gentleman should
never permit the lady to pay for refreshments.*

In entering a public room where ladies are present the gentleman should lift his hat.

If you accompany ladies to a theatre or concert-room, precede them to clear the way and secure their seats.

Do not frequently repeat the name of the person with whom you are conversing. It implies either the extreme of hauteur or familiarity.

Deference can always be better expressed in the voice, manner, and countenance that in any forms of words.

If when you are walking with a lady in any crowded thoroughfare you are obliged to proceed singly, always precede her.

Always give the lady the wall; by doing so you interpose your own person between her and the passers-by, and assign her the cleanest part of the pavement.

A gentleman should never permit the lady to pay for refreshments, vehicles, and so forth at public balls, theatres etc. If she insists on repaying him afterwards, he must of course defer to her wishes.

If you are smoking and meet a lady to whom you wish to speak, immediately throw away your cigarette or cigar.

Do not smoke shortly before entering the presence of ladies.

A young man who visits frequently at the house of a married friend may be permitted to show his sense of the kindness which he receives by the gift of a Christmas or New Year's volume to the wife or daughter of his entertainer.

It should be remembered that, without either ostentation or folly, a gift ought to be worth offering. It is better to give nothing than too little.

On the other hand, mere costliness does not constitute the soul of a present; on the contrary, it has the commercial and unflattering effect of repayment for value received.

A gift should be precious for something better than its price. It may have been brought by the giver from some far or famous place; it may be unique in its workmanship; it may be valuable only from association with some great man or strange event. Foreign curiosities, and the like, are charming gifts. An author may offer his book, or a painter a sketch, with grace and propriety.

Offerings of flowers and game are unexceptionable, and may be made even to those whose position is superior to that of the giver.

If you present a book to a friend, do not write his or her name in it, unless requested. You have no right to presume that it will be rendered any the more valuable for that addition; and you ought not to conclude beforehand that your gift will be accepted.

Never refuse a present unless under very exceptional circumstances. However humble the giver, and however poor the gift, you should appreciate the goodwill and intention, and accept it with kindness and thanks. Never say, 'I fear I rob you,' or, 'I am really ashamed to take it,' etc.

Such deprecatory phrases imply that you think the bestower of the gift cannot spare or afford it.

Never undervalue the gift which you are yourself offering; you have no business to offer it if it is valueless. Neither say that you do not want it yourself, nor that you should throw it away if it were not accepted. Such apologies would be insults if true, and mean nothing if false.

No compliment that bears insincerity on the face of it is a compliment at all.

If a person of greater age or higher rank than yourself desires you to step first into a carriage, or through a door, it is more polite to bow and obey than to decline.

Compliance with, and deference to, the wishes of others is the finest breeding.

When you cannot agree with the propositions advanced in general conversation, be silent. If pressed for your opinion, give it with modesty.

Never defend your own views too warmly. When you find others remain unconvinced, drop the subject, or lead to some other topic.

Look at those who address you.

*To yawn in the presence of others,
to lounge, to put your feet on a chair, to stand with
your back to the fire, to take the most comfortable seat
in the room, to do anything which
shows indifference, selfishness, or disrespect,
is unequivocally vulgar and inadmissible.*

Never boast of your birth, your money, your grand friends, or anything that is yours.

If you have travelled, do not introduce that information into your conversation at every opportunity. Anyone with money and leisure can travel.

The real distinction is to come home with enlarged views, improved tastes, and a mind free from prejudice.

Give a foreigner his name in full, as Monsieur de Vigny - never as Monsieur only. In speaking of him, give him his title, if he has one. Foreign noblemen are addressed *viva voce* as Monsieur. In speaking of a foreign nobleman before his face, say Monsieur le Comte, or Monsieur le Marquis. In his absence, say Monsieur le Comte de Vigny.

Converse with a foreigner in his own language. If not competent to do so, apologise, and beg permission to speak English.

Don't:

Don't wear anything but a silk hat with a frock or tail-coat.

Don't clean or cut your nails anywhere but in your own room.

Don't wear or use a collar or handkerchief that is not perfectly clean.

Don't take your invitation with you when you go to a private dance, nor forget to take it when you go to a public one.

Don't talk loudly or make much noise in trains or public places.

Don't push yourself into a train or bus before ladies.

Don't use a toothpick in public.

Don't eat or drink noisily.

Don't scrape your plate.

Don't forget to wipe your mouth after eating or drinking.

Don't turn your trousers up at the bottom unless
the streets are muddy, and if you have done so,
do not forget to turn them down on entering a room.
Don't moisten your fingers to turn over the
pages of a book.

Copper Beech Gift Books
are designed and printed
in Great Britain.